my itty-bitty bio

Michael Jordan

Published in the United States of America by Cherry Lake Publishing Group
Ann Arbor, Michigan
www.cherrylakepublishing.com

Reading Adviser: Beth Walker Gambro, MS, Ed., Reading Consultant, Yorkville, IL
Book Designer: Jennifer Wahi
Illustrator: Jeff Bane

Photo Credits: © Elena_Titova/Shutterstock, 5; © america365/Shutterstock, 7; © Duke Chronicle/Wikimedia, 9; © Jerry Coli/Dreamstime, 11, 15; © Gapvenezia/Wikimedia, 13, 22; © aimadbro/Shutterstock, 17; © Pete Souza/Wikimedia, 19, 23; © Everett Collection/Shutterstock, 21; Cover, 1, 6, 16, 18, Jeff Bane; Various frames throughout, Shutterstock

Copyright ©2022 by Cherry Lake Publishing Group
All rights reserved. No part of this book may be reproduced or utilized in any form or by any means without written permission from the publisher.

Cherry Lake Press is an imprint of Cherry Lake Publishing Group.

Library of Congress Cataloging-in-Publication Data

Names: Sarantou, Katlin, author. | Bane, Jeff, 1957- illustrator.
Title: Michael Jordan / Katlin Sarantou ; illustrated by Jeff Bane.
Description: Ann Arbor, Michigan : Cherry Lake Publishing, 2021. | Series: My itty-bitty bio | Includes index.
Identifiers: LCCN 2021007993 (print) | LCCN 2021007994 (ebook) | ISBN 9781534186866 (hardcover) | ISBN 9781534188266 (paperback) | ISBN 9781534189669 (pdf) | ISBN 9781534191068 (ebook)
Subjects: LCSH: Jordan, Michael, 1963---Juvenile literature. | Basketball players--United States--Biography--Juvenile literature. | African American basketball players--Biography--Juvenile literature.
Classification: LCC GV884.J67 S37 2021 (print) | LCC GV884.J67 (ebook) | DDC 796.323092 [B]--dc23
LC record available at https://lccn.loc.gov/2021007993
LC ebook record available at https://lccn.loc.gov/2021007994

Printed in the United States of America
Corporate Graphics

table of contents

My Story 4

Timeline 22

Glossary 24

Index 24

About the author: Katlin Sarantou grew up in the cornfields of Ohio. She enjoys reading and dreaming of faraway places.

About the illustrator: Jeff Bane and his two business partners own a studio along the American River in Folsom, California, home of the 1849 Gold Rush. When Jeff's not sketching or illustrating for clients, he's either swimming or kayaking in the river to relax.

my story

My name is Michael Jordan.

I was born in New York City.
It was February 17, 1963.

I love sports. My favorite is basketball. I played in college. I was part of Chapel Hill's team in North Carolina.

What sports do you like to play?

We made it to the **NCAA championship** in 1982. I scored the winning jump shot.

I joined the Chicago Bulls team in Illinois. This was in 1984.
I played 13 seasons with them.
I won six **NBA championships**.

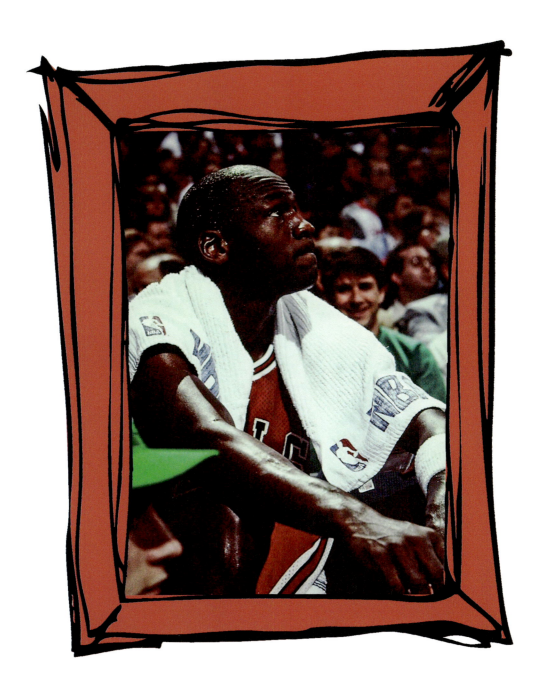

I played on the **Olympic** "Dream Team." We won a gold medal in 1992.

I am one of the greatest basketball players. I won many awards.

I worked with Nike to create the Air Jordan. These shoes were released in 1985. They are still popular today.

What kind of shoe would you create?

I like giving back. I work with the Make-A-Wish Foundation.

I received the **Presidential Medal of Freedom** in 2016.

I want to **donate** more than $100 million dollars. I want this money to go toward education and **social justice**.

What would you like to ask me?

timeline

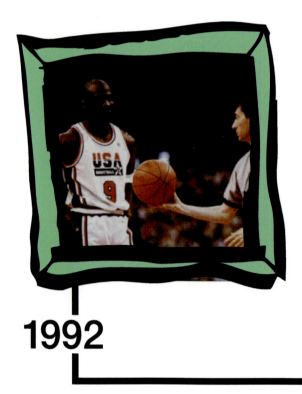

1992

1950

Born
1963

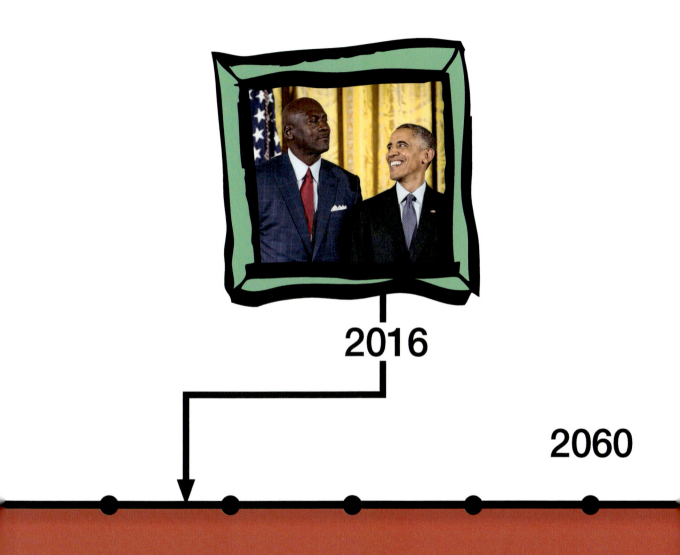

glossary & index

glossary

championship (CHAM-pee-uhn-ship) a final game in a sports series

donate (DOH-nate) to give money for a good cause

NBA (EN BEE AY) the National Basketball Association

NCAA (EN CEE AY AY) the National Collegiate Athletic Association

Olympic (oh-LIM-pik) a part of the Olympics, an international sporting event

Presidential Medal of Freedom (preh-zuh-DEN-shuhl MEH-duhl UHV FREE-duhm) an award given by the U.S. president to recognize a person's contributions

social justice (SOH-shuhl JUHSS-tiss) fairness when it comes to money and opportunities

index

Air Jordan, 16

basketball, 6, 14

championships, 8, 10

Chicago Bulls, 10

Dream Team, 12

Illinois, 10

NBA, 10
NCAA, 8
New York City, 4
Nike, 16
North Carolina, 6

Olympic, 12

social justice, 20
sports, 6, 7